FLORISTS' REVIEW

101

one-hundred-and-one

HOW-TO
FAVORITES

PUBLISHER: Frances Dudley

EXECUTIVE EDITOR: Talmage McLaurin

COPY EDITOR: Shelley Urban

PHOTOGRAPHY: Stephen Smith

FLORAL DESIGN: Talmage McLaurin
Bill Harper, AIFD
Carolyn Shepard, AIFD
Patrick Wages

Text excerpted from *Florists' Review* magazine,
written by David Coake, Editor-in-Chief and
Shelley Urban, Managing Editor.

Florists' Review's 101 How-To Favorites
was designed and produced by
Florists' Review Enterprises, Inc.;
3641 SW Plass; Topeka, Kansas 66611-2588

Printed in the United States by The John Henry
Company, Lansing, Michigan.

Separations and Postscript services by
Capital Graphics, Inc., Topeka, Kansas.

Design and Typesetting by Artemis,
Topeka, Kansas.

ISBN: 0-9654149-6-5 (*English*)
0-9654149-7-3 (*Spanish*)

FLORISTS' REVIEW

one-hundred-and-one

101

HOW-TO
FAVORITES

contents

romantic notions   6

spring celebrations   42

faux designs   82

sympathy tributes   88

corsages   102

wedding bouquets   108

autumn bounty   148

halloween   176

christmas   182

1 Use spray adhesive to attach single ivy leaves to a cardboard heart. Coat with a surface sealer when complete.

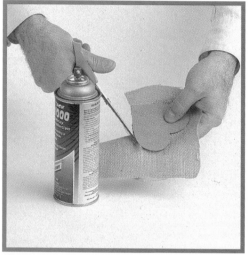

2 To cover a heart with burlap, spray a cardboard heart with adhesive and press on the burlap. Trim the edges with scissors and repeat the process to cover the reverse side.

3 Spray adhesive will also adhere tin foil to a cardboard heart to match foil-wrapped candy kisses. Crinkle the foil to match the texture.

Handmade hearts customize floral gifts for romantic occasions.

add-on hearts

SPECIAL HEART-SHAPED ADORNMENTS, which can be made in advance of the busy Valentine's Day holiday, add a touch of romance to fresh flower offerings. Whether you add burlap hearts, foil hearts, or the fresh ivy-leaf hearts shown here, your floral designs are instantly ready for romance.

Incorporate the hearts into your designs in creative ways, either on card holders, attached to basket handles, or tacked to vases as was done with these cylinder designs. Despite the common notion that hearts are more feminine accents, these three heart options—burlap, foil, and ivy—could be suitable for both male and female recipients.

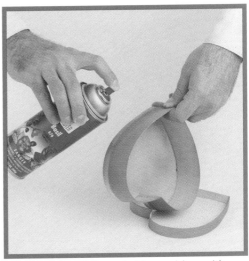

1 Spray a heart-shaped chipwood box with basil green paint.

HOW-TO **2**

A profusion of spray roses in a heart-shaped box is a sweet gift for sweethearts.

pavé roses in heart box

THE FLORISTS' ANSWER TO THE RUN-of-the-mill box of chocolates, this creative gift makes a big impact at an affordable price. A heart-shaped chipwood box which, along with its lid, has been sprayed with basil green paint, is lined with plastic and filled with wet foam. A lavish collection of affordable spray roses are arranged in the foam while moss and snippets of huckleberry provide a decorative edge. Since most spray roses are fragrant, this gift, a fabulous offering for Valentine's Day, is as sweetly scented as any box of chocolates and there's no guessing about the fillings.

2 Line the box with plastic, fill with wet foam, top foam with moss, and arrange roses.

3 Arrange snips of huckleberry around the edge of the heart box, then tuck the tips into the arrangement.

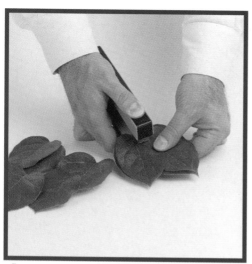

1 Start forming a collar of salal leaves by overlapping two salal leaves and stapling them together.

2 Continue overlapping and stapling leaves until a collar is formed. Be sure to leave a hole in the center.

3 Place the collar over the mouth of a vase and arrange tightly bunched waxflowers in the vase.

This economical floral gift is equally suitable for Valentine's Day or every day.

waxflower posy

WITH THE CURRENT POPULARITY OF compact arrangements, posy compositions should be well-received by consumers. In this stylish violet-inspired posy, a delicate cluster of tiny waxflower blossoms is accented by salal leaves to create a charming bouquet for expressing one's love without breaking the bank. Similar posy-style designs can be created using nearly any type of flower and, therefore, can be created in practically any price point, so there's a posy to suit your best customers, whomever they might be.

1 Spray an inexpensive cherub with gold metallic paint.

4

Spray roses and a simple accessory result in a lavish-looking design at an affordable price.

bed of roses

THE LATERAL STEMS OF PASTEL PINK spray roses, which have been clipped from the main stem, are individually arranged in moss-covered floral foam, creating a miniature "bed" of roses in a small ceramic urn. Combined with sprigs of ivy and a few stems of pink larkspurs, placed vertically to frame the gilded cherub, the spray roses create a full-flowered appearance with just a few stems. An excellent cash-and-carry design, this arrangement delivers maximum impact for a minimum price.

2 Hot-glue the cherub to the edge of a small urn. Spritz the urn with gold paint to match the cherub.

3 Fill the urn with wet foam, cover with moss, and arrange flowers.

1 Select a thick piece of moss and, using a heart-shaped pattern, cut out a heart.

Preserved pansies on a moss backing convey romantic sentiments with keepsake value.

moss and pansy heart

TIMELESS CLASSICS WITH INCREDIBLE colorings, pansies are spectacular when preserved. Although they present some design challenges with their flat constitution and lack of stems, pansies can be fashioned into delicate designs such as those shown here. When affixed to a heart-shaped piece of moss or foam, preserved pansies make glorious keepsake gifts for Valentine's Day.

2 Glue cardboard to the back side of the moss and glue pansies to the front with spray adhesive.

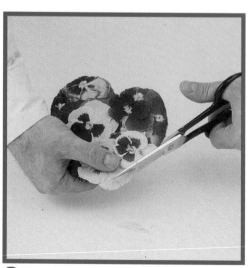

3 Allow the pansies to extend over the edge of the moss heart, then trim the edges with scissors.

1 Start wrapping a Styrofoam® heart form with sheer ribbon. Secure the ribbon ends with small straight pins.

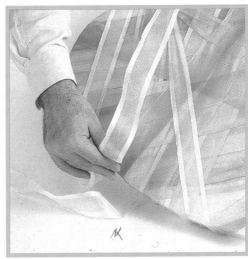

2 Continue wrapping the foam heart with varying colors and patterns of ribbon until it is completely covered.

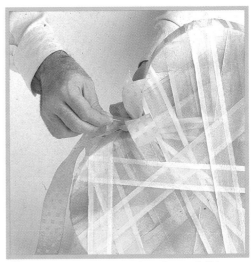

3 Hang the heart with a long loop of ribbon which is pinned into the top of the heart. Attach a bow at that same point.

HOW-TO 6

Ribbon-wrapped hearts invite customers into your shop.

ribbon display hearts

ENVELOPED WITH THE SHEER WRAP-pings of beautiful ribbon, these heart-shaped hangings are sure to capture attention, whether hanging in display windows or throughout your shop. In either case, these hanging hearts are perfect for filling the open space from the ceiling to the top of a display, especially a tabletop display of all your Valentine's Day specials.

Made quickly from either solid Styrofoam® heart shapes or hollow foam heart forms, these display hearts are simply wrapped with entire bolts of ribbon which can later be unwrapped and reused. Long loops of ribbon, attached with straight pins to the hearts' centers, hang the hearts with sheer beauty.

1 Cut a heart from cardboard and apply spray adhesive to one side.

2 Lay short pieces of chenille stems across the heart.

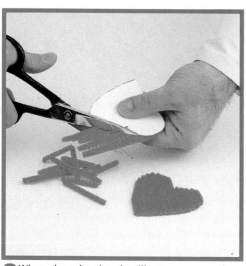

3 When dry, trim the chenille stems around the heart pattern.

Differentiate your shop's in-store specials with a simple yet attractive handmade accessory.

chenille heart

WHETHER YOU'RE CREATING A Valentine's Day arrangement or an in-store special for romantic occasions, a colorful chenille-stem accent will creatively distinguish your designs. Just apply the chenille stems to a cardboard heart with spray adhesive and affix the heart to the container. Create your chenille hearts in solid colors or in many colors and use them to accent containers featuring florals in coordinating colors.

HOW-TO 8

Creative canvases make a seasonal backdrop for Valentine's Day merchandise.

canvas heart panels

CREATE DISPLAY MASTERPIECES FOR Valentine's Day with artists' canvases, available at craft and hobby stores. Using a cardboard heart cut-out and several colors of spray paint—silver, purple, and red in this case—these three-dimensional display props are quickly completed. Although the canvases are mounted on sturdy boards, they are manageably light-weight and can be hung, propped up, or even displayed on easels. Once the heart art is in place, add an assortment of your shop's gift merchandise and floral designs to complete the traffic-stopping window display.

Although the canvases may cost $10 to $20 each, depending on size, they can be repainted and reused again and again. It's best to buy the board-mounted canvases in more than one size, both to add visual interest to your window display and so smaller ones can be used to carry the display concept inside your store.

1 Cut a heart-shaped "stencil" from sturdy cardboard. Lay it on a framed canvas and spray over it with silver paint.

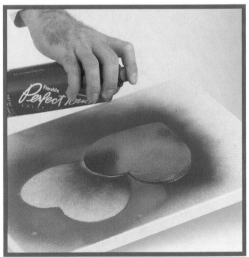

2 Move the heart stencil to another position on the canvas and spray over it with purple paint.

3 Move the stencil again and spray over it with red paint. The stencil can be sprayed over with each color in more than one position.

1 Tie a two-loop bow with wide satin ribbon.

2 Glue the bow on a glass vase with a dot of hot glue.

3 Hot-glue a gold-painted wooden heart in the center of the bow.

A lavish gathering of roses and some well-chosen accents send a loving message at a reasonable price.

bow-tied vase

FEATURING SEVEN STEMS OF DIFFER-ent spray rose varieties in each, these glorious arrangements are long-lasting gifts for romantic occasions. Presented in up-to-date fashion with wide Dior-style bows and gold-painted craft store hearts, these sure sellers offer easy assembly for Valentine's Day, anniversaries, and more. And as is common with many spray rose varieties, these roses should have a sweet fragrance that will please any recipient.

HOW-TO 10

A great idea for creating one-of-a-kind containers with a trendy look for holidays, special events, and every day.

ribbon weave vase

USING GLASS OR PLASTIC CYLINDER vases and an assortment of ribbons, you can capitalize on the resurgent popularity of handcraft and folk art by creating a series of woven patchwork containers which are exclusive to your shop. By vertically and horizontally interlacing a variety of patterns, fabrics, and widths of ribbon, you can easily and quickly produce a series of handmade vessels—each unique—and customize them for specific holidays, seasons, or special events. What a great way to use ribbon remnants and roll ends!

1 Place a rubber band around the rim of a cylinder vase. Under the rubber band, tuck strips of various ribbons which hang to the bottom of the vase.

2 Weave other pieces of ribbon horizontally between the vertical strips, alternating under and over the vertical strips. Connect the ends of the horizontal strips with hot glue.

3 Remove the rubber band. Secure the top and bottom ends of the vertical ribbons to the vase with dabs of hot glue or double-face tape.

1 Spray a terra-cotta pot with antique gold paint.

A simple treatment transforms an ordinary clay pot into a fabulous container.

gold-leaf pots

IN THEIR RICH GOLD-LEAFED TERRA-cotta pots, these mounded arrangements of vibrant red roses make modern statements about your shop and are quick pick-ups for hurried customers. For keepsake-quality floral gifts, use preserved roses like these exquisite selections, or for an offering of fresh cut florals, select red rose varieties in dark red hues. Although they're ideal for Valentine's Day sales, these rose-filled pots are appropriate decoratives year-round.

2 Apply a coat of spray adhesive and pat on sheets of gold leaf.

3 When the glue is dry, brush off excess gold leaf with a soft cloth.

12

Flowers arranged in concentric rings will appeal to today's savvy consumers.

miniature carnation biedermeier

PAINTED POTS OF PRETTY MINIATURE carnations, arranged in concentric rings, send stylish Valentine's Day love messages, yet they're priced right for budget-conscious beaus. Create several versions of these mounded arrangements in several color harmonies and with different or unusual varieties of miniature carnations. Especially wonderful for Valentine's Day, compact designs are appropriately sized for desk placement and are easy to deliver.

1 Fill a painted clay pot with floral foam and arrange a row of carnations around the rim of the pot.

2 Arrange a row of pink carnations inside the outer row and fill the center with white carnations.

3 Wrap a length of ribbon around the lip of the pot and tie a bow under the outer ring of carnations.

Create keepsake gifts with preserved floral materials.

tulle and rose pomander

POMANDER BOUQUETS OF PRESERVED roses and hydrangeas are welcome options for Valentine's Day. Easily constructed by hot-gluing the blossoms between loops of multiloop tulle bows, these versatile bouquets can be carried, hung in a special spot, or displayed on a pretty tray. Because pomanders are traditionally aromatic, consider adding a few drops of fragrant oil to each of the roses; a sweet scent will enhance the keepsake value of these exquisite gifts.

1 Make a bow from six-inch wide tulle. Continue adding loops until the bow resembles a ball.

2 Tie off the tulle ball with a length of tulle that will form the handle of the pomander.

3 Hot-glue preserved roses and hydrangea florets onto and between the loops of tulle.

HOW-TO 14

Decorate unadorned containers with playfully painted hearts.

wooden heart accents

ACCESSORIZE YOUR ROMANTIC GIFT offerings for Valentine's Day or any day with brightly painted die-cut wooden hearts. Here, two trendy citrus colors accent the traditional Valentine's Day pink. This color combination gives the arrangements a playful, modern flair and enables designers to incorporate nontraditional colored flowers. Both everyday and novel containers get a lighthearted lift from these fanciful additions. The hearts are available, unpainted, in a variety of sizes at craft stores everywhere.

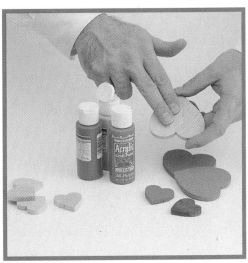

1 Paint various sizes of inexpensive wooden hearts with bright colors of craft paint.

2 Stack three large hearts and glue them to the bottom of a vase. Add a couple to the side as well.

3 In random placements, glue painted wooden hearts to the sides of natural wicker baskets.

1 Using an artist's knife, cut a heart shape from a piece of thick cardboard.

Elegant in its simplicity, this design offers options for romantic occasions.

carnation heart design

WHETHER ENHANCED BY FOLIAGE or left unadorned, this heart-shaped carnation design is a perfect table decoration for romantic celebrations. The pillow-like heart is fashioned of fluffy, long-lasting carnations which have been glued to a cardboard form. If foliage is to be added, be sure to use a shiny-leafed selection for greatest impact.

2 Using spray adhesive or low-temp. pan-melt glue, secure carnations on their sides around the edge of the heart.

3 Fill in the middle of the heart with the remaining carnations, gluing them upright.

HOW-TO 16

Decorative, custom-made shapes accent casual containers.

felt heart pails

TO CREATE A VALENTINE'S DAY GIFT with a retro look, try colorful felt. When cut into the desired shapes, felt can be easily adhered to almost any smooth-surfaced container. However, the felt's soft texture and matte colors are a nice contrast to the high-gloss enameled metal pails shown here. In addition to its affordability, another benefit to using felt is that it can be color coordinated with whatever flowers are readily available.

1 Cut squares in two sizes from pieces of red, pink, and purple craft felt.

2 From the same three colors of felt, cut heart shapes which are smaller than the small square.

3 Glue the pieces of felt in layers to the side of the container with spray adhesive.

1 Gather bunches of purple sinuata statice into a compact nosegay.

2 Add a collar of preserved *Galax* and bind with waxed string.

A traditional romantic gift receives an update for today's consumers.

faux violets

FEW FLORALS ARE AS REMINISCENT of the romantic Victorian era as posies of fresh violets. Although sweet violets are still available in the United States today, the growing season is limited and quantities can be hard to come by. Today, statice can be used as a hardy alternative to violets while providing a similar color and massed look. Here, stems of dried statice are clustered around a freeze-dried rose and edged with preserved galax leaves for an attractive yet more affordable option.

3 Accent with ribbons or add a preserved rose in the center.

HOW-TO 18

Two-tone clay pots are hot buys for cost-conscious consumers.

painted pots

A SIMPLE ARRANGEMENT OF STANDARD carnations, rimmed by a collar of Holland ruscus (*Ruscus aculeatus*), is showcased in perfect-for-summer style in these brightly painted clay pots. Priced at less than $30, arrangements like these are a tremendous value because they are designed in floral foam (the pots are lined with floral plant liner), and they will last and last.

1 Spray-paint the rim of a clay pot in the color of your choice and allow to dry.

2 Cover the rim of the pot with masking tape and spray-paint the body of the pot with a contrasting color. Allow to dry.

3 Fill the pot with floral foam. Add a "collar" of ruscus leaves and arrange standard carnations in the center.

1 Spray a half-dozen egg carton with basil green paint.

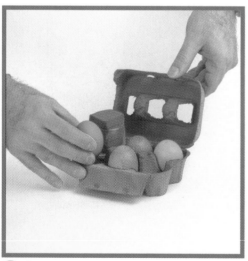

2 Hot-glue a votive candle cup into one of the egg compartments and fill with wet foam.

3 Fill the other compartments with dyed eggs or plastic eggs.

Fresh eggs and fresh flowers are cleverly combined for an enticing springtime arrangement.

egg carton arrangement

A CLEVER DESIGN FOR EASTER OR any springtime event, this small gathering of florals is arranged in a half-dozen-size egg carton and appears to have been delivered by the Easter bunny himself.

To arrange the flowers in the egg carton, a small votive candleholder, filled with wet foam, is hot-glued into one of the egg compartments, and the florals are simply arranged in the foam. The fresh eggs, which have been hard-boiled and colored in Easter fashion, can be dyed to coordinate beautifully with any variety of spring blossoms. For greater convenience, plastic eggs may be used.

HOW-TO 20

Modish backdrops that you can create in minutes.

napkin-covered screen

CREATING IMAGINATIVE BACKDROPS for window and tabletop displays is simple, quick, and affordable with foam-centered board and festive paper napkins. The napkins can be attached to the foam-centered board (which has been scored and folded to be free-standing) with straight pins or decorative thumbtacks.

With the innumerable designs on napkins today, backdrops like this tabletop screen can be made for virtually any holiday, season, or occasion. The rooster-and-hen motif featured here is ideal for spring and Easter displays. This display idea is also great for creating hanging banners to carry a theme throughout the store.

1 Score a sheet of foam-centered board vertically with an artist's knife to create the first panel of the screen. Make sure that the panel is slightly wider than the napkins.

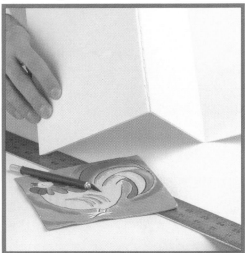

2 Turn the board over and score it again, creating another panel the same width as the first. Continue scoring on alternate sides so that the board will fold in accordion fashion.

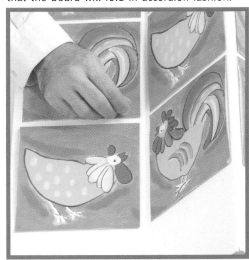

3 Attach napkins to each panel with straight pins or thumbtacks. If pins are used, push them all the way through the board and snip them off flush with the board's back side.

1 Draw stems and leaves on a piece of foam-centered board and cut them out with an artist's knife.

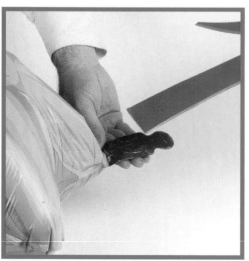

2 Spray both sides of the foam-board stems and leaves with glossy green paint.

3 Tape helium-filled daffodil balloons to the stems. "Plant" them in pots topped with soil.

Oversized, helium-filled balloons invite customers into your shop to buy a bit of springtime.

daffodil balloon display

GIANT DAFFODIL-SHAPED BALLOONS announce to customers and passersby that spring has arrived inside your shop, regardless of the weather. To create the stems and foliage, cut the shapes from foam-centered board and spray them with green paint. Then, simply tape the balloons' tabs to the "stems" and "plant" the foil daffodils in soil-filled, oversized clay pots. Accent the display with some of your shop's potted daffodils and other spring bulb offerings. Additional balloon daffodils can be placed around the store—near more potted bulb flowers and near the cooler—to draw attention to your cut spring flower selections.

1 Place a bunch of curved-stemmed tulips in a water-filled cylinder vase.

HOW-TO 22

A gardeny gathering of springtime florals is sure to delight any recipient.

bunched tulip arrangement

IN A RICH-LOOKING BUT AFFORDABLE rectangular plastic cylinder vase, a quick-to-design arrangement is created *sans* floral foam. A bunch of 10 tulips, the stems of which are still banded at the bottom, is placed in the vase and positioned on the rim. Between the tulips' stems, roses and foliage are arranged while a ribbon accent softens the design's off-center placement.

This pretty gift is wonderful for Mother's Day, and it is sure to please for both special occasions and everyday needs as well.

2 Arrange roses and foliage between the tulip stems.

3 Secure a bow and streamers to a wooden pick and add it to the design.

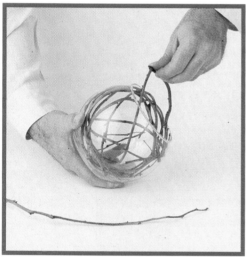

*A grid of natural
materials allows flowers
to be quickly and
sturdily arranged
in glass containers.*

bubble bowl mechanics

FOR THOSE WHO AVOID ARRANGING flowers in clear glass containers, we offer a simple technique which holds the flowers securely in place while allowing their stems to be seen. It also adds an interesting dimension to the arrangement.

A grid, much like lengths of tape crisscrossing the mouth of a vase, is created by "lacing" 8 to 10 bare salal stems (or other pliable stem or branch material) into the container. Flowers and foliage are then arranged through the grid. Because the salal stems are supple and pliable, the grid allows some flexibility in arranging yet provides the necessary tension to hold the florals in place. The resulting arrangement has a contemporary flair that will appeal to today's sophisticated flower buyers.

1 Remove the leaves from several salal stems. Slide the stripped stems around the inside of a bubble bowl.

2 Add stems until a "grid" is formed with the stems crisscrossing the opening of the bowl.

3 Fill the bowl with water and arrange tulips in the openings between the natural grid of stems.

24

Create a natural, gardeny setting to display your shop's floral designs.

moss-covered props

USING A FEW INEXPENSIVE HOME furnishings and some sheet moss, you can impart a decorative home appeal to both your fresh and permanent floral designs. In this display setting, an old chair, an inexpensive wooden column, and a discarded frame—all readily identifiable home decoratives—are covered with sheet moss in a topiary-like display. The sheet moss, which can be "refreshed" by mists of water mixed with moss-green acrylic craft paint, will last for months, enabling the display to be useful for several seasons.

1 With a paint stir stick or a paint brush, spread pan melt glue onto a small section of the surface to be covered.

2 Apply moss to the glue-covered area and press into place. Work in small sections, so the glue won't harden before application.

3 Wrap the moss with monofilament or florist's twine to further secure the moss to the form and to reduce its shedding.

Add natural realism to your clay pot creations with an easy paint technique.

faux-aged pot

ESPECIALLY SUITABLE FOR GARDEN-style arrangements and potted plants, this simple paint treatment yields a realistic, faux-aged finish. It takes just a few minutes to complete and the paint treatment adds a natural, gardeny feel to your potted gifts. Here, a faux-aged clay pot is topped with a glass dome to showcase a miniature geranium in terrarium style.

1 Spray a clay pot with soapy water, followed immediately by a coat of whitewash paint.

2 While the first coat is still wet, spray on more soapy water, followed by a coat of moss green paint.

3 While the second coat is still wet, spray on more soapy water, followed by a coat of basil green paint. Let dry.

HOW-TO

26

Capitalize on a hot trend with aquatic- inspired designs.

water garden

LARGELY BECAUSE OF THE ZEN-LIKE tranquility they impart, aquatic gardens, or water gardens, are the trendiest and fastest- growing segment of America's gardening rage. Distinctive arrangements inspired by this latest trend can be created in the flower shop by incorporating floating aquatic plants with cut florals and foliage.

This small water garden design features several aquatic plants, including water mint (*Mentha*), water hyacinth (*Eichhornia*), frog's- bit (*Limnobium*), and duckweed (*Lemna*). Stems of pokeberry (*Phytolacca*) and spider plant (*Chlorophytum*) foliage are arranged at the base so that they appear to be aquatic plants as well. Creating the height in this arrangement are sedges and grasses, umbrella palm (*Cyperus*), and lily grass (*Liriope*).

1 Using adhesive clay or hot glue, secure a small container filled with floral foam to the bottom of a water-tight planter.

2 Fill the planter three-fourths full with decorative gravel, small rocks, or smooth river stones.

3 Arrange cut botanicals in the floral foam and float aquatic plants in the water.

1 Dip an embroidered handkerchief in a solution of one-half water and one-half white glue.

A low-cost handkerchief adds value with pretty embroidered flowers.

hankie vase

A SIMPLE CLEAR GLASS VASE IS beautifully transformed with an inexpensive handkerchief that has been soaked in a solution of water and clear-drying glue (like Elmer's glue). The handkerchief adds color to an otherwise colorless container and lends a certain old-fashioned appeal to this low-cost creation. Overflowing with pretty flowers, this embellished-vase design makes a sweetly sentimental gift for both mothers and grandmothers.

2 Pat out the excess glue-and-water solution and tie the folded-in-half handkerchief around the neck of the vase.

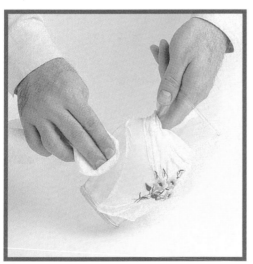

3 Allow the handkerchief to dry in place. Clean off any excess glue with a damp cloth prior to filling the vase with flowers.

HOW-TO 28

A fresh flower topiary design with a built-in water reservoir.

waterable topiary

INCORPORATING WATER RESERVOIRS into fresh flower topiary designs has been a challenge for many florists, and because of the lack of water, these popular designs have been impractical for occasions other than parties and similar short-term events.

In this design, however, the florals are arranged in a plastic Revere bowl filled with wet floral foam. The Revere bowl, which has a sizeable capacity for water, is camouflaged with moss and mounted atop the topiary trunk. A piece of plastic foam glued to the base of the Revere bowl allows it to be impaled on the topiary trunk. Recipients of designs like these can easily add water to the bowl, and because of the water reservoir, the florals will last as long as they would in a traditional arrangement.

1 Snap off the base of a plastic Revere bowl. Using pan melt glue, attach a small piece of plastic foam to the base of the bowl.

2 Cover the bowl and any exposed foam with moss, using spray adhesive to attach the moss to both the bowl and the foam.

3 Impale the foam-bottomed bowl onto a multibranch twig topiary stem. Fill the bowl with wet foam and arrange fresh florals.

Celebrate springtime with this pretty basket-style design.

butterfly basket

PERFECT FOR ANY SPRINGTIME occasion, including Secretaries' Day and Mother's Day, this cheery basket-style topiary proclaims spring's arrival. A faux-aging technique—spraying the pot alternately with paint and soapy water—adds a garden-planted feel to the pot, which is ringed with a heather (*Erica spp.*) wreath. The wreath, as well as the arching "handle," is formed by wiring strands of heather together. Topping the pot is a premossed ball, to which the heather "handle" is secured, and butterfly accents complete the delightful spring creation.

1 Bind several stems of heather with wire and form into a wreath the same diameter as the opening of the pot.

2 Secure wreath to the rim of the pot with hot glue and place a moss-covered ball in the pot. Attach an arch of heather over the top of the ball.

3 Attach butterflies of your choice to the moss-covered ball with a few drops of hot glue.

HOW-TO

30

Arranging permanent flowers to resemble their fresh counterparts.

permanent flowers and fresh bulbs

THE REALISM OF TODAY'S botanically correct permanent bulb flowers can be enhanced by arranging them (and their foliage) as close to the way they grow as possible. And when designing pots of permanent bulb flowers, that means that bulbs might be visible.

In this design, stems of fabric tulips (which closely resemble the 'Spring Green' viridiflora cultivar) are inserted through real tulip bulbs and into moss-covered foam—achieving the ultimate in realism and botanical correctness. The blooms and foliage are then positioned naturally to mimic live potted tulips.

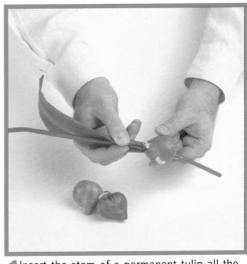

1 Insert the stem of a permanent tulip all the way through a fresh bulb.

2 Arrange several of the tulip-pierced bulbs in a planter containing moss-covered foam.

3 Arrange additional bulbs (without tulips) on top of the moss-covered foam as needed and as space allows.

A wire wreath form provides a stable base for permanent floral designs.

moss-base wreath

ARRANGED IN A WIRE WREATH FORM packed with moss, an analogous collection of fabric garden flowers composes a sumptuous wreath, the beauty of which can be enjoyed from spring through summer. The florals are designed in a natural style to have an almost planted, growing appearance. The mossed wreath form is a sturdy base that is wonderfully suited for the design of permanent florals and other weighty items requiring stability when hung on a door or wall.

1 Pack a wire wreath form tightly with moist sphagnum or sheet moss.

2 Wrap the mossed form with waxed florists' twine.

3 Arrange permanent botanicals directly into the moss.

HOW-TO 32

Both decorative and supportive, a bamboo structure enhances fresh floral designs.

bamboo "trellis"

ARRANGED TO APPEAR GARDEN-planted, these unruly but cheery yellow tulips are contained in an ordered fashion by a simple bamboo "cage." In addition to being a decorative element, the cage encourages the flowers to grow upward and outward. Cut succulents, seeded eucalyptus, and deciduous huckleberry add an untended-garden look at the base of the arrangement.

1 Place three bamboo stems vertically into a foam-filled pot. The stems should flair outward slightly.

2 Bind three short pieces of bamboo horizontally to the vertical pieces, a few inches from the top, with lengths of raffia.

3 Arrange fresh tulips inside the bamboo "trellis" and add assorted foliage to the base of the design.

1 Spray antique gold paint on a damp sponge.

2 Wipe the surface of a clay pot with the sponge.

3 Glue a bow-shaped charm to the center of the pot.

Affordable adornments create unique, trendy containers.

charmed pot

WITH A BRASS CHARM FROM THE local craft store and a wash of gold paint, an everyday terra-cotta container is easily transformed into a contemporary high-fashion vessel.

For Mother's Day, a shiny bow was chosen to adorn the pot although many different charms could be used for other holidays, special occasions, and even everyday designs. The pot, which is filled with floral foam, showcases pretty pastel-colored spray roses and miniature carnations. A covering of moss disguises the foam and minimizes the need for foliage which, in turn, gives the design a clean, modern look.

Use a simple towel treatment to add a special touch to a relaxation-themed gift basket.

terry cloth rosette

A GIFT OF INDULGENT BATH AND beauty products is sure to be a hit with those in need of a relaxing break from the stresses of home and office. Hand towels formed into rosettes add to the pampered effect as well as help hold the items in place. A casual, carefree gathering of florals is perfect for a basket of such pretty pleasures. While men might appreciate the relaxing benefits of such a special gift, this indulgent offering is especially suited for women.

1 Form a rosette at the end of a hand towel by rolling one edge. Tie off the rosette just under the "bloom" with taped wire.

2 Using double-face tape, secure the towel around the inside edge of a plastic tray with the rosette positioned on the edge of the tray.

3 Secure a clear glass cylinder and a variety of bath/spa products in the center of the tray with double-face tape.

A novel design with gardeny charm.

clay pot topiary trunk

SMALL CLAY POTS FORM THE CLEVER "trunk" of this garden-inspired topiary. The florals, which include soft yellow miniature gerberas (germinis) and golden yellow roses, are complemented by tufts of blue-violet hydrangeas and are arranged in the top pot of the stack. A variety of foliages contributes to the design's informal gardeny appeal.

1 Hot-glue a stack of three-inch clay pots in the center of a six-inch clay pot filled with floral foam.

2 Secure the stack by inserting a length of bamboo through the drainage holes of the small pots and into the foam.

3 Hot-glue an inverted pot to the top of the stack, and glue on two saucers to hold a small block of floral foam.

36

Leftover stems help to form a gardeny topiary design.

gladiolus stem topiary

AN EXQUISITE SPRINGTIME GIFT selection, this multi-hued rose and ivy topiary is perfect for Mother's Day, special occasions, and more. Gladioli stems comprise the trunk of the sophisticated creation, while the fresh materials are arranged in an Iglu Holder which is hot-glued atop the bundle of stems. Many types of fresh florals and foliage could be used to create pretty topiaries in several price points.

1 To form a topiary trunk, insert gladiolus stems into a foam-filled clay pot.

2 Trim all the stems to an even height. Hot-glue an Iglu Holder to the top of the bundle of stems.

3 Arrange fresh roses and ivy in the Iglu and place moss at the base of the trunk.

An affordable yet glamorous arrangement for wedding receptions and other special occasions.

baby's breath topiary

BABY'S BREATH, VALUED TODAY AS more than just a fresh flower filler, offers an affordable alternative for customers seeking contemporary reception and party designs.

Here, a half bunch of baby's breath is banded together and placed in a clay pot which has been filled with moss-topped floral foam. The stems form a natural trunk for the abundant collection of blooms. Ribbon, selected to coordinate with the special event décor, is braided around the stems.

Whether in pairs on a mantle or decorating every table in the room, baby's breath topiaries are suitable for many types of events—from casual gatherings to the most formal affairs.

1 Bind the stems of a half bunch of baby's breath with taped wire at the top and bottom.

2 Starting three inches from the bottom, wrap stems with ribbon, crossing the ribbon and twisting it against itself.

3 Tie a bow at the top of the stems and insert the ends of the stems into a foam-filled clay pot.

38

A footed stand enhances the traditional bubble bowl.

rose bubble bowl

TRANSFORMING A SIMPLE BUBBLE bowl design into an elegant gift with Asian flair is easily and quickly accomplished with the addition of a classically styled teakwood stand. Glued to the bottom of the bubble bowl, the teakwood stand elevates the rose arrangement and imparts a fine-quality feel at an affordable price.

1 Affix a piece of duct tape to the bottom of a glass bubble bowl and hot-glue it to a wooden stand.

2 Affix another piece of duct tape to the inside bottom of the bowl and hot-glue a small piece of floral foam to it.

3 Arrange fresh roses and eucalyptus foliage in the foam and fill the bowl with three-fourths of an inch of water.

1 Mix acrylic water according to instructions and pour into a clear glass cylinder.

2 Bend chicken wire over the opening of the vase to hold flowers in place.

3 Arrange flowers in the base. When liquid hardens, cut away the wire.

Create amazingly lifelike designs with this new design tool.

acrylic "water" vase

ACHIEVING A REALISTIC, ALMOST-natural appearance with permanent arrangements is possible today with the fine crop of high-quality products on the market. Contributing to the realism afforded by botanically correct florals is acrylic "water," which, although it looks like water, actually hardens, holding permanent floral materials in place for years.

Here, a gathering of fabric gerberas, arranged in a clear glass cylinder vase, makes an impressive and eye-catching home interior design. In the acrylic water, these loosely arranged gerberas are as lifelike as can be.

1 Fill a glass canning jar or fruit jar with artificial fruit.

40

Use acrylic "water" for more than just fabric flowers.

faux preserves

ESPECIALLY USEFUL FOR CREATING lifelike home accents, acrylic water can be used with practically any type of permanent botanicals. Here, permanent fruits are used to create trendy "preserves," which make attractive decoratives for counters, shelves, or open cabinets. Simply place any permanent fruits or vegetables into old-style canning jars and pour the acrylic water mixture into the container.

2 Add acrylic water, following the manufacturer's instructions.

3 Wedge a ball of chicken wire into the jar to hold fruit in place until liquid hardens.

Natural stems and realistic-looking florals combine for a lifelike home decorative.

permanent topiary

A LUSH, ABUNDANT TOPIARY OF lilacs, hydrangeas, zinnias, and lotus pods, in green hues from light and bright to dark and shadowed, imparts a fresh, summery feeling to any environment. With an almost rectangular form and a characterful multi-stem trunk, this composition is doubly stunning when used in pairs on a mantel, buffet, or dining table. The fresh stems and moss base enhance this design's realistic appearance.

1 Insert sturdy willow branches into a pot filled with dry foam. Cover the foam with moss.

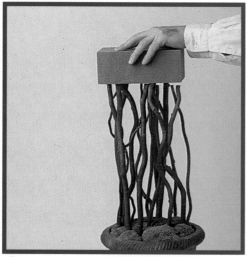

2 Trim tops of willow stems evenly and press a block of dry foam on top.

3 Arrange botanicals in the dry foam. Cover any exposed foam with moss.

42

This novel, custom-designed container is perfectly suited for a wildflower-inspired tribute.

leaf-covered basket

WHEN A DISTINCTIVE CONTAINER IS desired for a special sympathy design, how about transforming a traditional plastic sympathy basket with a covering of fresh foliage? In this case, salal leaves, generously coated with spray adhesive, do the trick.

In such a natural container, gardeny or wildflower-like blossoms are the logical choices. An abundant assortment of filler-type flowers create the wildflower look while line and mass flowers, in contrasting colors, create accent and depth in the design.

1 Spray a plastic sympathy basket with moss green paint.

2 Spray floral adhesive to the backsides of individual salal leaves.

3 Starting at the bottom of the basket, press the leaves on in overlapping rows.

1 Using taped wire, secure a floral foam cage in the center of a wicker fireside basket.

2 Arrange flowers in one end and the top of the holder. Save the cut stems.

3 Arrange the cut stems in the opposite end of the foam so the flowers appear to be laying in the basket.

A casual arrangement style becomes a memorable tribute.

sympathy gathering basket

MAKING AN UNCOMMON expression of sympathy, brightly colored flowers and perky gingham ribbon are arranged in a traditional fireside basket to resemble cuttings from a summer garden. A floral foam cage, secured in the center of the basket, keeps the flowers fresh. The lower portions of the stems are inserted horizontally into one end of the foam cage while the blooms are arranged in the other, so the flowers appear as if they're just laying in the basket.

1 Insert the ends of long pieces of myrtle and *Leptospermum* into a floral foam wreath form.

44

Swirling branches give a rose-covered wreath an air of distinction.

foliage swirl wreath

THIS SOFT, GARDENY WREATH, constructed in a wet floral foam form, is distinguished by the swirling motion created with a collection of flowering and leafy branches. The branches are arranged in the foam first, almost completely covering the wreath form. Snippets of assorted foliages, which bring textural variety, are then added to finish covering the form. Finally, a combination of spray and hybrid tea roses is placed around two-thirds of the wreath, which leaves visible the dynamic circular lines created by the branches.

2 Remove blooms and foliage from the tip of each piece and insert each tip into the foam, following the circular wreath form.

3 Add snippets of foliage to the wreath to cover any gaps. Finish the wreath by adding flowers and a bow.

1 Place a moss-coated wreath form on top of a floral foam cross form at the intersection of the crossbar and the shaft.

2 Secure the wreath to the cross by wiring in the four places where the wreath and cross touch.

3 Attach mossed twigs around the edges of the cross with heavy-gauge hairpin wires.

Two foam forms are combined for a loving tribute that expresses family heritage.

celtic cross

A TRADITIONAL RELIGIOUS SYMBOL for those of Irish, Scottish, or Welsh descent, the Celtic cross, which has a ring that intersects the shaft and crossbar, is an appropriate sympathy tribute. However, without a standard foam form in the shape of a Celtic cross, a little design ingenuity is required.

Here, a wreath form, which comes already coated with moss, is attached to the front of a traditional cross-shaped floral foam form, yielding a base in the desired shape. The florals, in colors which echo the serene beauty of stained glass windows, are arranged in the foam cross, while natural branches enhance the moss-coated wreath. Together, the two forms combine for a gorgeous, heritage infused tribute to a loved one.

1 Cut each stem of lilies in half and arrange the blossoms in one end of a foam cage.

HOW-TO 46

A new sympathy style popularized by one of Princess Diana's casket pieces.

gathered bouquet

LIKE THE SIMPLE SPRAY OF TULIPS that gracefully adorned the coffin of Diana, Princess of Wales, this single-flower set piece could also be laid as a tribute on a casket or burial plot. For a hand-tied appearance, the lilies' stems are cut short, and the blossoms are arranged in the top of a foam cage while the remaining stem portions are inserted into the bottom. Foliage is added to conceal the cage, and ribbon is attached where a binding point would normally occur on a hand-tied design.

2 Arrange the leftover lily stems in the opposite end of the holder.

3 Add foliage, then attach a bow where a binding point would be if this was a hand-tied design.

1 Wire several stems of heather together into four bundles and insert all eight ends into the foam cross to form a four-section circle.

2 Arrange small pieces of foliage around the edges of the cross. Be careful to avoid covering too much of the heather ring.

Another technique for creating the traditional tribute.

celtic cross

THIS VERSION OF THE CELTIC cross—a cross that is shaped like a traditional Latin cross but which has a ring that intersects the shaft and crossbar—is created on a standard foam cross form, and the ring is fashioned entirely of Scotch heather. The woody stems are inserted directly into the sides of the foam shaft and crossbar.

3 Fill in the body of the cross with carnations, spray roses, waxflowers, and foliage. Place on an easel for presentation.

48

Two sympathy icons form a contemporary tribute.

carnation and wheat wreath

BISECTING A SUMPTUOUS WREATH of fluffy carnations and eliminating the need for a traditional bow, a sheaf of fresh green wheat symbolizes the prosperity and riches of a full life. Designed in a wet floral foam wreath form, the approximately 100-125 carnations will remain fresh for several days. Although beautiful when hung in a traditional manner on an easel, this tribute is even more distinctive when laid on a casket.

1 Cover a wet floral foam wreath form with carnation heads.

2 Bind a sheaf of wheat just under the heads.

3 Attach the sheaf to the wreath with Dixon pins or wire.

1 Tie several small ribbon bows, securing them with taped wire.

2 Place the bows together to form a teardrop shape. Secure with floral tape.

3 Using Oasis Floral Adhesive, glue individual blossoms and snips of foliage into the loops of ribbon.

This easy-to-assemble corsage is lightweight and comfortable for the wearer.

glued corsage

IN ADDITION TO THE TRADITIONAL methods of corsage construction, lightweight corsages can be made by gluing flowers and pieces of foliage into a base of ribbon loops using Oasis Floral Adhesive or low-temp. glue. This delicate corsage of Michaelmas daisies (*Aster novi-belgii*) and oregonia, for example, was constructed with glue rather than wire and tape and is easily worn on even the most lightweight spring and summer fabrics. When gluing corsages, avoid hot-melt glue; it can damage the flowers, and when it becomes cold during refrigeration, flowers and foliage may "pop" loose.

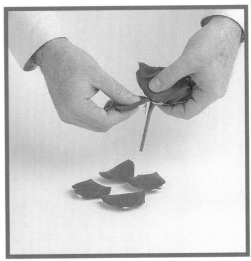

1 Remove several outer petals from a rose to create "rosebuds" for the tip of the corsage.

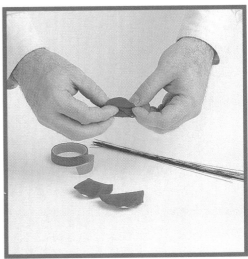

2 Roll each petal to form a small "bud" and secure each with two crossed wires. Tape each stem.

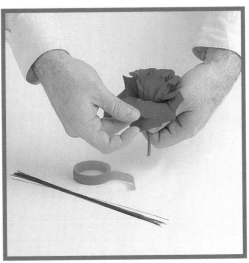

3 Allow the rose to reach room temperature and gently reflex each petal to achieve an open-bloom look.

HOW-TO 50

An easy-to-wear style for Mother's Day, proms, and weddings.

reflex-rose corsage

A SINGLE ROSE IS ALL THAT'S needed to create this understated, modern-style corsage. After four of the outermost petals are removed to create the "bud" at the top of the corsage, several of the remaining outer petals are gently reflexed to achieve the appearance of an open rose. When using fresh rose foliage, it is advisable to spray it first with an antitranspirant, some of which are formulated especially for cut greens and cut flower foliage.

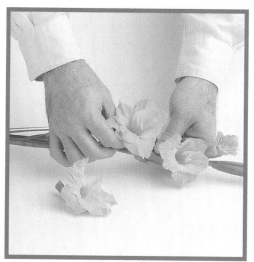

1 Remove the florets from one *Gladiolus* stem. Spray the florets with an antitranspirant.

2 Slice through one side of each floret and remove pistils and stamens. Nestle the florets one inside the other, from the smallest to the largest.

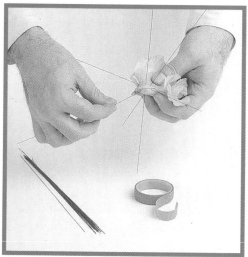

3 Insert four wires through the bottom of the nestled florets. Bend the wires down and wrap with floral tape.

A fabulous floral accessory appropriate for today's fashions.

glamellia

TO REKINDLE CONSUMERS' DESIRE for corsages, florists must design modern styles which are easy and comfortable to wear and which accessorize but don't overpower today's fashions. A glamellia corsage, made with varying sizes of *Gladiolus* florets, will accomplish all of these goals.

Forgotten or feared by many florists but fascinating to most consumers, elegant glamellia corsages are actually easy to construct and highly profitable. This perfect-sized corsage contains florets from only one stem of *Gladiolus*. A beautiful color-coordinated silk ribbon enhances the ruffled elegance.

52

Creating a "designer" look for a common bouquet holder gives bouquets added elegance and distinction.

torch handle bouquet

SINCE MANY OF TODAY'S BRIDAL bouquets are designed in plastic-handled bouquet holders, creatively differentiating your bouquets from those of other florists will instantly set your wedding work apart. Here, a straight-handled Wedding Belle Bouquet Holder is camouflaged with a shantung silk-covered piece of poster board which is formed into an elegant conical handle for the bouquet. Beautiful gold cording just beneath the bouquet disguises the holder's foam cage. While it opulently accessorizes the bouquet, the new custom-designed handle is also larger than the original plastic handle and is, therefore, easier for jittery brides and maids to hold.

1 Cut out a wedge-shaped piece of poster board. Using spray adhesive, cover one side with fabric. Form a cone and hot-glue the two edges together.

2 Hot-glue several short strips of poster board around the top inside edge of the cone. Coil metallic cord to cover this area and secure it in place with hot glue.

3 Saturate the foam of a straight-handled Wedding Belle Bouquet Holder. Then, hot-glue the bouquet holder inside the fabric-covered cone. Avoid getting poster board wet.

1 Arrange permanent roses in the center of a Lomey Dry Foam Bouquet Holder and form a collar with individual loops of ribbon which are attached to wooden picks.

2 Create ribbon roses by folding a piece of #40 ribbon in half lengthwise and tightly rolling the ribbon in the center and getting looser as the rolling continues.

3 Wire the rolled ribbon rose at one end and tape with stem wrap. Arrange the ribbon roses among the silk blooms in the nosegay.

New permanent flowers with delicate, sheer petals add a romantic aura to bridal bouquets.

ribbon rose nosegay

YOU ALMOST HAVE TO LOOK TWICE to notice that the beautiful cream-colored roses in this stylish nosegay are not fresh. And with a closer look, you'll notice that the petals are fashioned of both sheer and opaque fabrics, creating softly feminine flowers which are perfect for wedding bouquets. The dainty café-au-lait-colored rosebuds interspersed among the off-white roses are created with the same elegant satin-edge moiré ribbon which accessorizes the bouquet. And instead of foliage, individual loops of that ribbon are placed to produce a sumptuous ruffly collar around the bouquet.

HOW-TO 54

Novel leaf-wrapped clusters of baby's breath compose an affordable bridal bouquet.

blossom and leaf bouquet

WHEN THE BRIDE REQUESTS something delightfully different yet affordable, this understated nosegay, comprising small clusters of 'Million Stars' baby's breath wrapped in *Galax* leaves, would be an imaginative option. If other colors are desired, the wired-and-taped "pockets" of posies can also be fashioned with tufts of acacia, waxflower, *Leptospermum*, heather, or any other small-blossomed filler flowers. Fanciful loops and tails of sheer, wire-edged ribbon and a lovely Victorian-inspired posy holder, which beautifully conceals the wired-and-taped stems, finish the bouquet in an appropriately delicate fashion.

1 Place a small cluster of baby's breath in the center of a *Galax* leaf and wrap the leaf around the cluster in a cone shape.

2 Pierce the *Galax* leaf cone near the bottom with a thin wire and tape with green stem wrap.

3 To assemble the bouquet, gather several of the *Galax* leaf cones and tape them together. Continue adding cones to complete the bouquet.

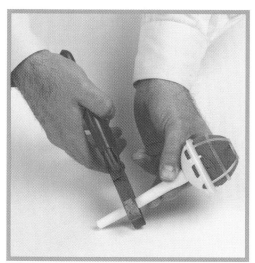

1 Shorten the plastic handle of a straight-handle bouquet holder to about three inches in length by cutting it with wire snips.

2 After arranging flowers in the bouquet holder, position the shortened handle in the center of the doily and tie a chenille stem around the top of the handle.

3 Secure the doily in place by inserting hairpin-shaped chenille stems into the foam in several places around the underside of the bouquet.

Add an elegant detail to an exquisite compact bouquet.

doily-backed nosegay

SMALL, COMPACT BOUQUETS REMAIN the vogue among brides today. With color in the floral materials and delicate enhancements to the design, the posy style can be simple while also lavish. This dainty nosegay of pink roses and seeded *Eucalyptus*, nestled in an exquisite Battenburg lace doily, exemplifies the trend toward small yet finely detailed bouquets.

HOW-TO 56

Add stylish detail to a simple bouquet design.

leaves and lace

A COLLAR OF LACY LEAVES IS A pretty way to dress up a monochromatic collection of miniature carnations, transforming the simple nosegay into a stylish bouquet for brides and maids. For additional interest, a few of the lace-covered leaves are arranged amid the flowers. While all-white designs are popular choices with many brides, lace-enhanced leaves can be pretty additions to today's colorful bouquets as well, especially those in pastels. Despite the detailed look achieved, covering the leaves is an easy task.

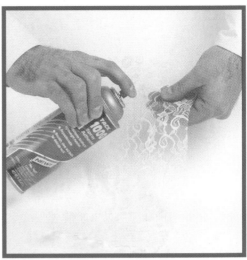

1 Apply spray adhesive to a piece of lace fabric or ribbon.

2 Firmly press salal leaves face down onto the lace.

3 After the adhesive has dried, cut the leaves out of the lace.

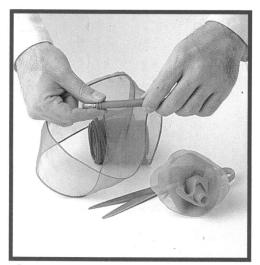

1 Tightly wrap several layers of wired ribbon around a pencil. A sheer organza or chiffon works best.

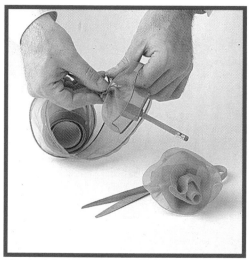

2 Continue wrapping the pencil, adding folded pleats at the bottom and causing the top of the ribbon to flare.

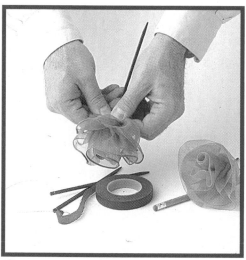

3 To create a stem, wire the finished rose to a wired wood pick and wrap with florists' tape.

A delicate ribbon rose becomes a cherished keepsake in a bouquet of fresh blossoms.

ribbon rose

TRADITIONAL IN SHAPE ONLY, THIS ultra-feminine bouquet has a thoroughly modern feeling. Trendy blossoms in vividly contrasting colors, a "web" of silver bullion, and a distinctive ribbon treatment combine to create a special bouquet for today's brides and maids.

A keepsake ribbon rose, which can be retained as a remembrance of the momentous event, occupies a prominent but off-center place in the design. A bouquet holder is crucial to maintaining the freshness of the flowers, especially the super-thirsty hydrangea tufts.

58

Add a designer touch to a stylish bouquet with a simple decorative accessory.

cone handle bouquet

PACKED WITH FRAGRANT BERRIED juniper and concealing a straight-handled Wedding Belle Bouquet Holder in its center, a decorative metal mesh cone, originally intended to hang on the wall as a decorating accent, becomes an arty handle for a sophisticated winter wedding bouquet. The modish handle gives the bouquet a cutting-edge couture style. And on the practical side, the cone can be inserted into a foam-filled base of foliage or flowers to create a contemporary topiary-like centerpiece for use following the ceremony.

1 Fill a decorative wire mesh cone with bits and pieces of fresh berried juniper.

2 Nestle a straight-handled, presaturated Wedding Belle Bouquet Holder into the center and wire in place.

3 Create the bouquet by arranging flowers in the foam of the bouquet holder.

1 Form a heart shape from heavy-gauge wire which is covered with floral tape. Wrap the wire heart artfully with ribbon.

An elegant bouquet for the romantic at heart.

heart frame bouquet

A DELICATELY FEMININE CLUSTER OF hybrid tea roses, arranged in a Wedding Belle Bouquet Holder and framed by a heart-shaped ribbon-and-bullion-covered wire form, is a stunning and modern option for Valentine's Day brides or those desiring a sweetly romantic bouquet at any time of the year. It's also a more affordable and gardeny alternative to the solid heart-shaped rose bouquets which have been the vogue in recent years.

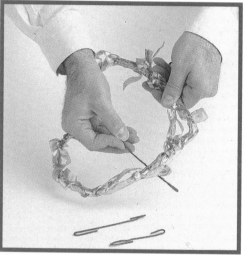

2 Form three hooks out of floral-taped heavy-gauge wire. Bend both ends of each hook and clip one end of each hook onto the wire heart.

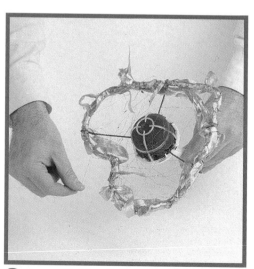

3 Place a Wedding Belle Bouquet Holder in the center of the heart and insert the three wire hooks into the holder. Secure with a wrapping of gold bullion.

HOW-TO 60

A fresh, new concept in bridal bouquets.

elongated orchid pomander

MONOBOTANICAL BOUQUETS ARE stylish choices for today's brides and maids, as are the more compact styles which accent the attire rather than obscure it. This elongated pomander bouquet, a totally contemporary style for brides, is a stunning example of a small yet exquisite bouquet. Created with a range of green *Cymbidium* orchids, this elongated bouquet is excellent for spring and summer nuptials. To form the bouquet, individual blossoms are wired and taped and construction begins at the bottom.

1 Wire and tape two to three dozen individual *Cymbidium* orchid blossoms using a thin-gauge wire.

2 Starting with a single orchid, tape additional blossoms to form an elongated pomander.

3 Attach a loop of ribbon to the end of the bouquet to form a handle. Add additional loops for a bow.

1 Encircle a permanent open rose with bunches of permanent lilacs.

2 Knot a length of tulle at the base of the nosegay.

3 Wrap tulle around the outer edge of the nosegay to form a "cocoon."

A common request becomes a nosegay.

single rose nosegay

FOR THOSE FLORISTS WHO CRINGE when brides-to-be ask for single roses for their attendants, we offer this bouquet which provides a similar simplicity but with more panache, style, and profit.

A millinery-quality permanent rose, in a glorious stage of openness, forms the center of this nosegay and is surrounded by permanent lilacs in two subtle hues. Adding an ethereal veiled effect is a "cloud" of soft tulle into which the entire collection of blossoms is nestled. An equally delicate sheer striped ribbon completes the composition.

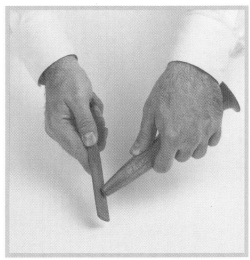

1 Unscrew the bottom of a candlestick and cut off the screw with a pair of wire cutters. File the area until it's smooth.

62

The vogue in bridal bouquets today is colorful, compact, gardeny and exquisitely detailed.

candlestick bouquet holder

WITH THE STAFF OF AN ORNATE metal candlestick for its handle, this globe-shaped bouquet of pale peach-colored roses has a stately elegance. Delicate star-shaped blooms of white *Bouvardia* are used as accent flowers between the roses. As both types of flowers are particularly "thirsty," they are arranged in a water-soaked Wedding Belle Bouquet Holder, the shortened handle of which is inserted into the socket of the candlestick.

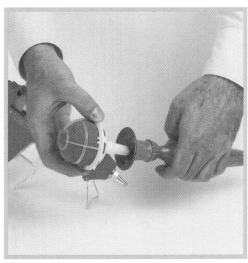

2 Adhere duct tape inside the socket of the candleholder. Hot-glue a shortened-handle Wedding Belle Bouquet Holder into the tape-lined socket.

3 Arrange flowers and foliage into the presoaked foam of the bouquet holder.

63

1 Wrap the handle of a Wedding Belle Bouquet Holder with brown floral tape.

A covering of curly willow transforms the traditional bouquet holder design into a nature-inspired nosegay.

twig armature

PERMANENT CURLY WILLOW, WITH a flexible wire center, is the key to this elongated bouquet holder with rustic inspirations. The permanent curly willow is wound to form a sturdy handle as well as a circular framework into which a foam-filled bouquet holder is firmly nestled.

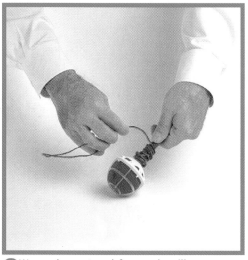

2 Wrap wire-centered faux curly willow branches around the handle until it is completely covered.

Preserved roses, which offer the bride a treasured keepsake remembrance from her special day, are accented by fresh materials including spray roses, *Bouvardia*, sprigs of ivy, and a few branches of fresh curly willow. Encircling the bridal composition are swirls of pheasant feathers, which echo the movement established in the curly willow formation and add a fall or winter feel to this very natural bouquet.

3 Continue wrapping until you've created a "halo" of willow around the foam cage.

1 Bundle several stems of *Equisetum* and bind them together in two or three places with rubber bands.

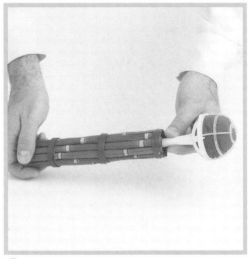

2 Cover the rubber bands with pieces of lily grass or raffia. Insert a straight-handled Wedding Belle Bouquet Holder into the bundle of *Equisetum*.

3 Arrange roses and foliage in the foam of the bouquet holder. Add a few loops of beautiful ribbon.

HOW-TO 64

A distinguished bouquet holder treatment provides more versatility for carrying.

handle enhancement

BECAUSE MANY A NERVOUS BRIDE and attendant relax the positions in which they hold their bouquets, the backsides of bouquets and the handles of bouquet holders are often unattractively captured in photographs. By decoratively enhancing a Wedding Belle Bouquet Holder handle with fresh floral materials, such as the horsetail reed used here, a number of problems are solved. Not only is the handle camouflaged, but it is lengthened and thickened, providing more ways in which the bouquet can be properly and comfortably carried. And with a collar of fresh foliage supported by beautiful velvet and matte-finish satin ribbons, there is not an unfinished or unattractive side to the bouquet.

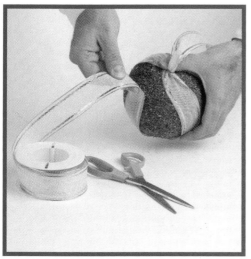

1 Wrap a length of ribbon around a moss-covered sphere, crossing the two ends at the bottom and dividing the ball into four sections.

2 Leave enough ribbon at the top of the ball to loop and tie into a handle.

3 Make small multiloop bows and attach them to the ball at the base of the handle. Using Oasis Floral Adhesive, glue fresh roses into the loops.

Create an attractive bouquet with a minimum of time and materials.

moss ball pomander

A MOSS-COATED FOAM SPHERE, a yard or so of ribbon, and a stem or two of spray roses are all the materials required to create this pretty pomander bouquet. Although beautiful for bridesmaids, this type of pomander design is a great choice for flower girls, as it will hold up well in the hands of even the most active children. The spray roses, which are glued into the bow with Oasis Floral Adhesive, will remain intact and easily withstand the stress of a long day. This bouquet is also lightweight and easy to carry and hold throughout the entire event.

Composed of the petals from many roses, a duchess rose bouquet is a royal selection fit for a queen.

duchess rose

WITH ROUNDED BOUQUETS EXPERI-encing a resurgence in popularity today, the duchess rose bouquet may be requested for formal weddings. Although the composite flower can be time-consuming to create and, consequently, costly for the client, discriminating brides will surely consider this exquisite bouquet worth the added expense. This duchess rose creation, composed of the petals from luxurious 'Madame Delbard' roses, is accented by an opulent collar of gilded leaves with a stunning result.

1 Wire two rose petals at a time with thin hairpin-shaped wires. Twist the wire at the base of the petal cluster.

2 Tape double petal clusters around a single rose blossom until the desired width is reached.

3 Add fresh or permanent leaves around the perimeter of the bouquet to support and protect the petals and finish the back.

Creative uses of grass-like foliage can add distinction to your bridal bouquets.

grass bouquet holder handle

1 Cut a moss-covered plastic foam ball in half and hollow out one half. Cut a hole in the center and insert the handle of a Wedding Belle Bouquet Holder through the hole.

2 Starting at the bottom, tape clusters of permanent grass onto the handle at three different positions, so that the second and third clusters overlap the first and second clusters.

THE "NEUTRAL" COLORS AND delightful casualness of this fragrant bouquet make it ideal for all kinds of spring and summer weddings. Loops of permanent grass, winding in and around the bouquet, add distinctive rhythm and dimension and appear to end in a feathery tuft, decoratively camouflaging the bouquet holder handle. Fresh foliage, such as bear grass (*Xerophyllum*) or lily grass (*Liriope*), can be substituted for the permanent material used in this bouquet.

3 Hot-glue short stems of permanent grass around the top of the handle, just beneath the ball, to cover the floral tape which secures the third cluster of grass to the handle.

HOW-TO 68

A favored flower arranged in a nontraditional manner.

rose cone bouquet

MODERN FASHIONS REQUIRE bouquets that are distinctive and equally modern. The conical bouquet, a new style in flowers to carry, is just such a bouquet. It can be crafted from almost any blossoms; however, roses are perhaps the most effective and the easiest with which to work. In this hand-tied bouquet featuring a trio of colors, construction begins with a single rose at the top which is surrounded by three roses on a slightly lower level. Additional roses are added at varying levels until a cone shape is achieved.

1 Remove the foliage from 24 to 36 long-stemmed roses. Cluster three roses around a single bloom and secure with floral tape.

2 Continue adding rows of roses to encircle and overlap each previous row. Add one or two roses to each new row until a cone shape is formed.

3 When the conical bouquet is completed, add a collar of permanent or fresh leaves at the base. Trim rose stems evenly and store bouquet in a vase.

1 Staple salal leaves around a bouquet collar in an overlapping pattern.

2 Trim the inside edges of the leaves and slide a small bouquet holder through the center.

3 Arrange flowers in a tight mass while still allowing the edging of leaves to be exposed.

Fresh foliage can be used to form a natural collar around a delicate bouquet.

leaf-collared nosegay

FRAMED BY A "RUFFLY" RING OF shiny green leaves, this softly colored posy-style bouquet has a decidedly Victorian feeling. Attached to a bouquet collar, the leaves can be angled to form varying sizes of bouquets which would be appropriate for flower girls and bridesmaids as well as brides. Streamers of elegant double-faced satin ribbon, with only a couple of loops, replace the traditional bow.

70

A contemporary styling for a traditional holiday wedding bouquet.

halo rose bouquet

A TRADITIONAL CHRISTMAS RED bouquet is given a modern and glittery personality when covered with a webbing of elegant gold bullion and surrounded by a golden "halo," gilded branches, and flourishes of metallic ribbon. Clusters of purple statice tucked around the edge of the bouquet add a rich regalness to the red and gold color scheme.

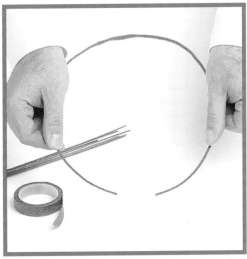

1 Shape a circular form with heavy-gauge wire which is covered with stem wrap tape.

2 Wrap the wire circle with ribbon. Add extra pieces of ribbon, tying knots and making loops around the halo.

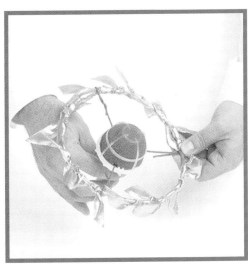

3 Center the halo around a Wedding Belle Bouquet Holder and attach with three wire hooks — one end inserted into the holder and the other clipped to the halo.

1 Cluster stems of baby's breath to form a dense nosegay and wrap the stems with floral tape.

2 Attach a wire stem to each *Stephanotis* blossom using replacement stems (such as Stay-Fresh Stephanotis Stems) or wire, cotton, and Parafilm.

3 Arrange the wire-stemmed *Stephanotises* through the baby's breath nosegay which will help hold the *Stephanotises* in place.

Featuring both Stephanotis and baby's breath, this elegant nosegay is a superstar selection.

stephanotis nosegay

WITH THEIR BRIGHT-WHITE, STAR-shaped lobes and sweet fragrance, *Stephanotis* is considered by many florists and consumers to be the quintessential wedding flower. Although they are available year-round, *Stephanotises* are most plentiful during the summer months, when most weddings occur. In this bouquet, we combined the favored wedding flower with another popular wedding selection, *Gypsophila*. The dense "cloud" of *Gypsophila* forms the foundation of this bright starry bouquet and creates a base through which the wired stems of *Stephanotis* are inserted. The baby's breath base gives the delicate *Stephanotis* blooms stability and holds them in place.

72

Handle treatment helps florists "get a grip" on affordable arrangements with high perceived value.

wheat sheaf basket

A BASKET WITH A LOW SQUARE handle is the ideal beginning to an affordable arrangement that achieves a full, high-perceived-value appearance with relatively few florals. The key is the handle treatment, which extends the design beyond the typical boundaries of the foam-filled basin.

In this case, the ribbon-tied stalks of wheat adorning the handle of this small wooden basket, actually an herb seedling box, are so pretty that the florals within the basket don't dare obscure them. Therefore, just a few fresh blossoms will fill the basket and provide a lavish-looking design with value-priced appeal.

1 Place two miniature sheaves of wheat in opposite directions atop the handle of a basket.

2 Secure the sheaves with a taped wire and disguise the wire with a tie of ribbon.

3 Fill the basket with wet floral foam and arrange fresh flowers.

1 Hot-glue a column of dry foam or Styrofoam® into a clay pot.

A year-round design technique with perfect suitability for fall.

grass stem topiary trunk

A COLUMN OF DRY FLORAL FOAM (or Styrofoam®) glued into the center of a simple earthen vessel forms the foundation of this topiary-style design which features leftover grain stems to hide the mechanics and form the topiary "trunk." Atop the grain stems, which are held in place by a rubber band disguised by raffia, permanent magnolias and various textural foliage are arranged in the foam column. Although this design clearly has a hint of autumn in its creation, the bundled-stem look has popular year-round appeal and is adaptable to many seasonal styles.

2 Surround the foam column with stems from grasses.

3 Arrange permanent florals in the top of the column.

HOW-TO

74

An autumn-inspired gathering of fruits and flowers.

pineapple and rose urn

THIS STATUESQUE DESIGN, IN ALL ITS textural splendor, is a graceful fountain of fall's finest fruits including 'Leonidas' roses, a cored pineapple, and a shower of grasses.

Although this creation is clearly autumn-inspired, it could be adapted to any season. For example, light-colored roses and a shower of fresh herbs could make it suitable for springtime.

1 Fill a cored-out pineapple with wet floral foam and arrange decorative grasses.

2 Insert wood picks into the bottom of the pineapple and place it into a foam-filled container.

3 Arrange fresh roses in the wet floral foam to adorn the base of the pineapple.

1 Using a wood pick, secure an artichoke into a foam-filled clay pot.

2 Pull back artichoke leaves at even intervals and add rose petals.

3 Continue until the desired look is achieved.

Celebrate the bounty of autumn with its fruitful offerings.

rose- petaled artichoke

ALMOST ARCHITECTURAL IN ITS styling yet ruggedly natural, this topiary-like artichoke arrangement is an innovative and long-lasting harvest-inspired design. Accessorized for fall with ocher-colored petals from a 'Leonidas' rose, this unusual-looking vegetable creation will sell best in multiples.

76

A lush gathering of fall's best and brightest fruits.

pumpkin cornucopia

IN THIS CONTEMPORARY cornucopia, ideal for a buffet or side table, honeysuckle vines appear laden with fall leaves and ripened pumpkins, gourds, and berries which have been "picked' into the design and wrapped with gold bullion. Floral materials embellish the arrangement with autumn-appropriate hues.

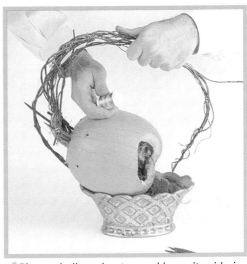

1 Place a hollowed-out pumpkin on its side in a foam-filled container. Insert a bundle of vines wrapped with gold wire into the bottom of the pumpkin.

2 Using wood picks, attach smaller pumpkins and gourds to the large pumpkin to form a cornucopia shape.

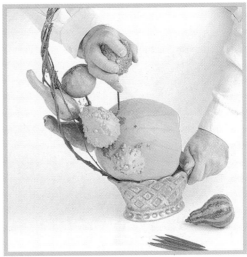

3 Finish the curved cornucopia form by hot-gluing moss, leaves, and berries into the vines. Place wet floral foam into the pumpkin and arrange florals.

1 Fill a hollowed-out pumpkin with wet floral foam. Arrange magnolia leaves around the edge and fill the center with zinnias.

2 Insert wood picks into the bottom of the pumpkin and place it into a foam-filled urn.

Undeniably autumn, this statuesque design is ideal for fall gatherings.

pumpkin urn

ATOP A STATELY URN, A RINGLET of oregonia and grass surrounds a hollowed-out pumpkin topped with magnolia foliage and a fall-hued mound of a zinnias. A shower of grass erupts from the zinnias, putting the finishing touches on this glorious multitiered arrangement.

3 Arrange foliage between the base of the pumpkin and the rim of the urn. Arrange a shower of grasses in the center of the zinnias.

78

Cute and cost-effective, these little designs are perfect for fall festivities, especially Halloween.

pumpkin pots

MOUNDS OF ORANGE CARNATIONS are arranged in wet foam inside faux-aged clay pots for fun and clever fall designs. Two salal leaves and a discarded flower stem, inserted into the foam through the center of the carnations, completes the pumpkin appearance with a stem-like effect. Despite their obvious Halloween application, these pumpkin pots are perfect decoratives for fall gatherings and autumnal entertaining.

1 Create a mound arrangement of tangerine carnations in a clay pot.

2 Place a carnation stem in the middle of the arrangement to create a faux pumpkin stem.

3 Arrange two salal leaves on both sides of the stem to resemble pumpkin foliage.

1 Bundle discarded wheat stems and bind on both ends with taped wire.

2 Hot-glue the bundle of stems into dry floral foam which has been placed inside a clay pot.

3 Hot-glue poppy pods and oak leaves to the top of the stem bundle to create a topiary design.

Natural elements form a creative, woodland-style topiary.

poppy pod topiary

LEFTOVER STEMS, ESPECIALLY THOSE of grains and grasses, make excellent topiary trunks. They are simply bundled together and banded at the top and bottom. For stability in the clay pot, the bundled stems are glued into the bottom and moss is tucked in around the stems. To finish the topiary design, Mediterranean oak leaves (*Quercus*) and poppy pods (*Papaver*) are glued onto the stems. This low-cost creation will sell well singly, but display it in multiples for affordable impulse sales.

80

Rings of materials give dried designs a modern look.

garland-rimmed rye bundle

BEFITTING A MODERN KITCHEN, A tricolor bundle of wheat (*Triticum*), placed simply in a footed glass cylinder, is appropriately banded with a premade garland of dried pumpkins (*Curcubita*) and bay leaves (*Laurus*). With its harvest-inspired colors and pumpkin accents, this shapely home accessory should last from early fall through Thanksgiving.

1 Mix three colors of rye together to create a large bundle.

2 Drop the multicolor bundle of rye into a clear glass vase.

3 Secure a premade garland of dried pumpkins and bay leaves around the bundle at the rim of the vase.

1 Push a clear acrylic Lomey Design Systems Column into the center of a foam-filled urn.

Distinctive candlelit decoratives for fall.

flowering candles

FEATURING FRESH FLORALS AND textured pillar candles, this distinctive duo makes an impressive in-home presentation during the autumn season. The florals, arranged in foam in distressed-finish urns, surround clear acrylic Lomey Design Systems Columns which support the trendy pillar candles. The candles can be removed for easier delivery.

2 Arrange foliage vertically around the column and wire it loosely to hold it in place. Next, arrange flowers.

3 Affix a pillar candle onto a Lomey Universal Piece with florist's clay and place it onto the top of the column.

HOW-TO 82

Everyday seasonal items are quickly fashioned into unique candle designs with high-end, decorator appeal.

autumn glow bowl

USING ELEMENTS COMMONLY FOUND in any flower shop, imaginative florists can create original candle designs for every season which are beautiful on dining tables, end tables, and mantels. This autumn composition showcases a pillar candle surrounded by dried miniature pumpkins inside a glass bubble bowl. An assortment of pods or other dried fruits would be equally enticing inside additional bowls for fall. Permanent leaves are glued randomly to the outside of the bowl, and a length of cording and more leaves provide a decorative touch to the base.

Although pillar candles are the best choice because they are designed to burn down inside themselves, it is important to avoid placing highly flammable dried materials inside the bowl.

1 Spray fabric leaves with adhesive and press them randomly onto the surface of a glass bubble bowl. Attach a few leaves to the base of the bowl also.

2 Place an inverted votive candle holder into the bowl and partially fill the bowl with small dried pumpkins and pods. Secure a pillar candle on top of the votive holder.

3 Hot-glue cording around the base of the bubble bowl. Display finished designs on decorative plates or trays to create additional sales.

1 Spray one side of fall-colored fabric maple leaves with adhesive.

2 When adhesive is tacky, press leaves in place on a moss-covered topiary form.

3 Arrange permanent berry and leaf branches at the base of the topiary.

Premade topiaries are ready to sell or to be quickly enhanced for added profits.

fall topiary

AMONG THE NEWEST AND COOLEST products exciting floral designers today are these premade, multiple-stemmed, moss-covered topiaries which are available in a variety of geometric forms. And although they're the ultimate in chic as is, they can be adorned in an infinite number of ways by creative florists. With little effort and additional product, this duo is enhanced with dried miniature pumpkins and permanent berries and leaves and can be sold individually or as a pair.

84

An unusual container adds a natural feel to this collection of dried floral materials.

chimney thimble arrangement

TODAY'S DIVERSE CROP OF DRIED and preserved materials enables florists to create in-home accents to meet any customer's needs. This notable dried design is no exception. Like an untouched field of wild flowers, this unkempt looking vegetative design of peonies, sea holly (*Eryngium*), tansy (*Tanacetum*), and dried grasses appears to grow naturally from a broken terra-cotta chimney thimble, the base of which is wrapped with moss.

1 Hot-glue a terra-cotta tray into the bottom of a clay chimney thimble.

2 Crack a piece out of the side of the chimney thimble and glue in a piece of dry floral foam.

3 Arrange florals in the foam and secure grasses in place around the outside with a band of raffia.

1 Lay a few inexpensive permanent leaves on a piece of brown kraft paper.

2 Spray paint lightly onto each leaf, letting the "over spray" create leaf outlines.

3 Move the leaves around and use different colors of paint until a desired pattern is achieved.

Quickly create a seasonal backdrop for window and in-store displays.

patterned backdrop

WITH KRAFT PAPER, SOME SPRAY paint, and a dowel rod, you can quickly and affordably create a seasonally eye-catching backdrop for window displays or in-store vignettes. Useful throughout the fall season, this colorful hanging backdrop is created with paints of various autumnal hues, each sprayed around a permanent leaf. The individual paint colors should overlap somewhat, resulting in a multilayered appearance. We used six different colors— blue, purple, orange, red, basil, and moss green.

Similar displays can also be created for holidays and other seasons. For Christmas, for example, red and green paint can be used to outline permanent holly and berries on white butcher paper. For additional outline materials, craft store stencils offer several options.

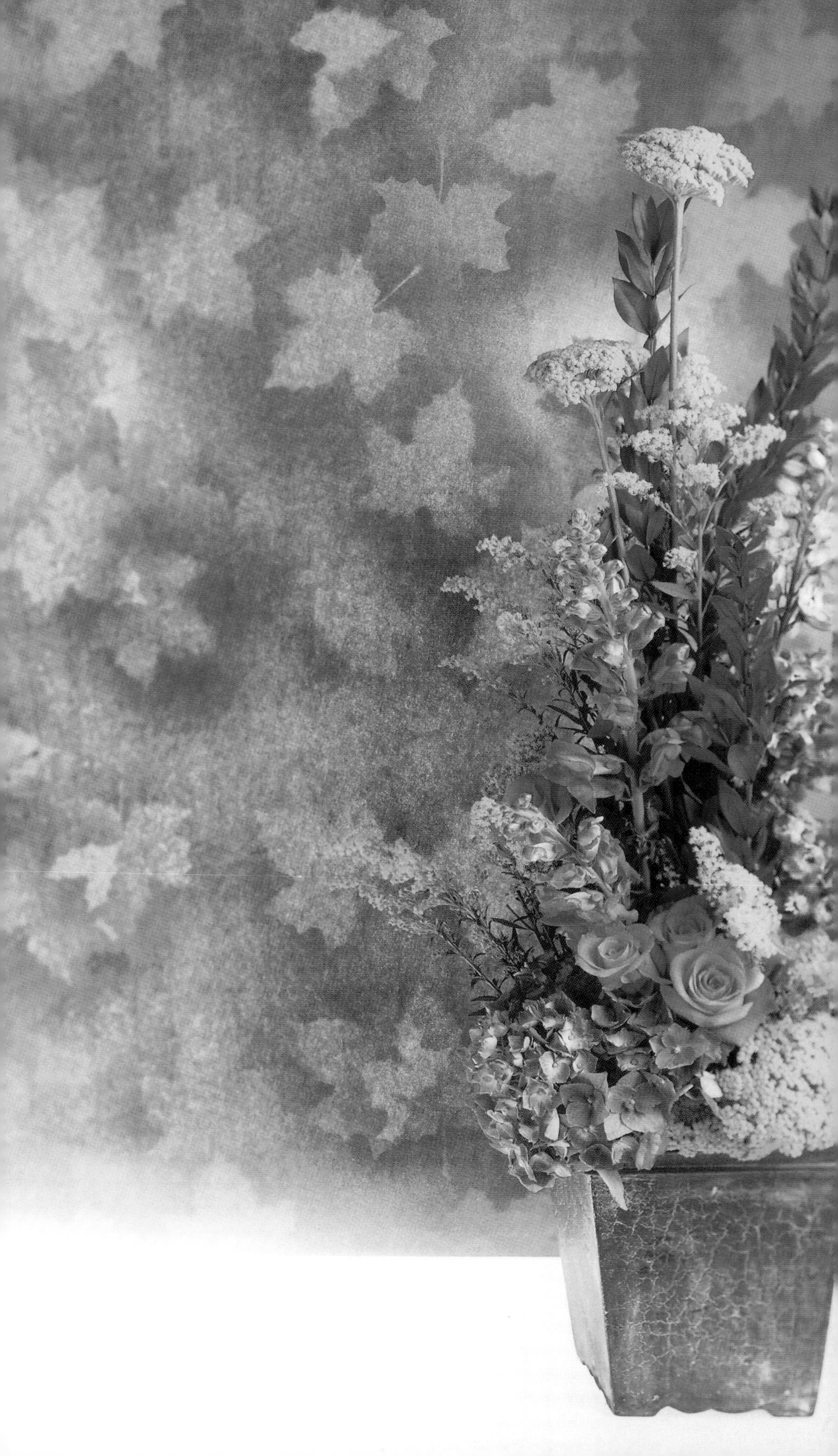

86

Use a few tricks to create Halloween treats for your customers.

handkerchief ghost

EVERY YEAR, AN INCREASING NUM-ber of adults go batty over Halloween. And by entrancing the spirited party-givers with bewitching bouquets, you'll surely scare up some extra sales at a most opportune time. For example, adding a little spirit to Halloween "boo-quets" is easy to do with a few white handkerchiefs, wooden candle extenders, and heavy-gauge wire. While the aforementioned items form the phantasmal bodies, google-eye-enhanced ball candles form each apparition's uppermost appendage. When these ghostly formations are positioned above any Halloween arrangement or plant, an instant candlelit centerpiece appears.

1 Drape a handkerchief over the end of a wooden candle extender. Wrap taped, heavy-gauge wire around one end to form "arms." Cover with another handkerchief.

2 Twist a chenille stem around the top of the candleholder. Then tie a folded handkerchief to cover the chenille.

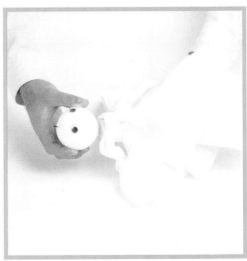

3 Secure a white ball candle to the top of the candleholder with double-faced tape.

1 Shape black chenille stems to resemble spider legs and hot-glue them to a cardboard disc.

2 Paint a clay pot black and glue on a cardboard disc which is decorated with eyes and a mouth. Hot-glue the pot to the spider leg disc.

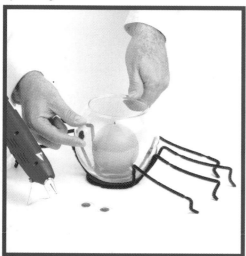

3 For a spider candle holder, hot-glue a small bubble bowl to the flat disc. Glue eyes to a ball candle or the outside of the bowl.

Add a little fun to your Halloween parties.

spider leg containers

TURNING EVERYDAY CONTAINERS, such as pots and bubble bowls, into an army of arachnids is a simple matter with black chenille stems—and you don't even need a witch's spell to do so. Just create a formation of multiple legs and nestle a container in the center. Then, simply drop an orange ball candle, to which google eyes have been attached, into the bubble bowl and fill the pot with assorted flowers or a plant.

Although both selections are delightful on their own, the pair, or several of each, make an inspired centerpiece when "crawling" down the center of a table. The effect of "witches' brew" boiling in the black plastic cauldron is created with a clever ultrasonic device which atomizes water, yielding a smoke-like mist.

1 Write "BOO" on the outside of a clay pot with a glue gun.

88

Halloween-enhanced terra-cotta pots make "terra-fying" seasonal containers.

"boo" pots

ARMED WITH HOT GLUE GUNS AND black spray paint, inventive designers can create a whole host of unique Halloween containers from naturally orange terra-cotta pots. Two containers, one with orange Halloween icons on black pots and the other with black images and words on orange pots, are created with a single drizzling of glue. When designed in varying sizes, these frighteningly clever arrangements will fit both the largest and smallest budgets. Cluster a series of them for a delightfully spooky centerpiece.

2 When the glue is dry, spray-paint the entire pot, glue and all.

3 Peel off the hot-glue letters to reveal the word "BOO." Attach the letters to an unpainted pot with spray adhesive.

1 Hot-glue a papier-mâché bowl to the center of a paint-treated terra-cotta tray. Place a row of apples around the mâché, and secure additional rows of apples with wooden picks.

2 Tuck tufts of moss into the spaces between the apples. Fill the papier-mâché container with wet floral foam which extends above the rows of apples.

3 Arrange fresh flowers and foliage in the wet floral foam, making sure the stems reach the bottom of the mâché container. At the last minute, add sliced kiwi fruit.

Arrange fruits and flowers beautifully for the holidays.

apple centerpiece

A LAVISHLY FRUITED CENTERPIECE, flanked by two coordinating candleholders, makes a delightful holiday table setting. The neutral-hued design, arranged in a low terra-cotta tray, features 'Granny Smith' apples, stacked and picked together for stability. A papier-mâché planter, filled with wet floral foam, is glued into the center of the tray, and the floral materials are arranged inside the planter. Bits of moss are used to fill in the base, and sliced kiwi fruits are added where needed for visual interest.

HOW-TO 90

Christmas traditions enhanced with pizzazz.

berry vase topiary

WHEN IT COMES TO CHRISTMAS decorations and arrangements, traditional styling is preferred by most consumers, but that doesn't mean that holiday designs can't have some originality. Here, traditional Christmas icons such as winterberries, evergreens, and red roses are arranged in a modern-day holiday manner using a vase-inside-a-vase technique, which provides a multitude of design options. Surrounding the center cylinder vase are *Ilex* berries which have fallen from their branches. Inside the cylinder is a hand-tied Biedermeier-influenced bouquet of roses to which statice, evergreens, and bare salal stems have been tied and hot-glued.

1 Place a small cylinder vase inside a larger wide-lip vase. Fill the space between the two vases with winterberries.

2 Form a nosegay of long-stemmed roses. Then glue pieces of statice and evergreens around the roses with Oasis Floral Adhesive.

3 Place the nosegay into the cylinder vase and brace it with salal stems from which the leaves have been removed.

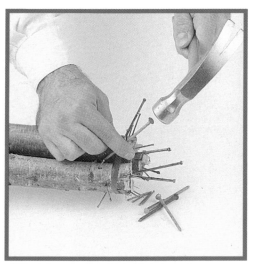

1 Bind four or five thick birch branches together at both ends with waterproof tape. At one end, hammer in several headless nails.

2 Fill a decorative container with dry floral foam or plastic foam. Hot-glue the bundle of birch branches into the foam-filled container.

3 Skewer apples and crab apples onto the nails. Hot-glue pieces of fresh fir into the spaces between the apples and crab apples.

Use this clever technique to create an impressive holiday design.

apple tree topiary

SEVERAL THICK BRANCHES ARE USED to compose a sturdy trunk for this holiday topiary, giving it an almost authentic "apple tree" appearance. Sprigs of fresh fir are glued in to seasonally enhance the design and fill in the space between the small crab apples and the flavorful 'Jonathan' apples, both of which have been skewered onto headless nails. Although they'll sell well as singles or with coordinating bowl creations, these fruited topiaries are likely to sell best in pairs.

92

A remarkable holiday creation for home or office.

holiday apple tree

WITH RINGS OF FRESH GREEN APPLES and a swirl of fragrant evergreens and festive red winterberries, this inventive topiary will no doubt be the talk of the town, whether at your Christmas open house or your best client's home or office.

The apples are situated on graduated sizes of wire wreath forms which are placed over the foam cone, which is purposely distressed for added character. Foliage and berries are inserted directly into the foam cone, and cleverly topping the "tree" is an inverted clay pot crowned with a foliage-and-berry-filled apple. A design which can be used indoors or out (imagine a pair flanking a client's front door), this arrangement can also be scaled down to mantel and tabletop sizes.

1 To texturize the surface of a large foam topiary form, randomly remove chunks of the foam with a knife, then spray-paint the form with moss green floral paint.

2 Slip graduated sizes of wire wreath rings over the top of the foam cone and lower each until it is firmly seated on the cone, making a series of circular "shelves."

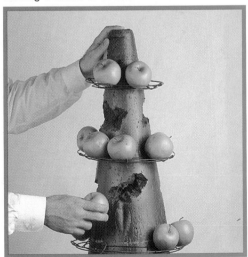

3 Place fresh green apples on the circular "shelves" and decorate the tree by arranging stems of berries and foliage directly into the foam cone in spiral fashion.

A seemingly profuse design that's actually light on materials and on the budget.

fruited candle

THIS CANDLELIT COLLECTION OF preserved pepperberries, permanent boxwood, miniature fruits, and fresh yarrow (that will dry in place) is a tremendous value and a super seller for the holiday season. Not only is this exquisite creation wonderfully suitable for Christmas, it would be appropriate for Thanksgiving as well. Although it appears to be abundant, this fruitful, della Robbia-inspired arrangement, which will sell easily in pairs, uses only snips of product to cover the moss-wrapped column of dry floral foam.

1 Fill a clay pot with dry floral foam so that the foam extends five or six inches above the rim of the pot.

2 Cover the foam with moss, securing it in place by wrapping waxed twine or paddle wire around it.

3 Arrange florals and ribbon in the foam. Attach the candle to the top of the foam with florist's clay.

1 Scrunch a long piece of wire netting (chicken wire) to form a narrow "tube."

94

An updated design technique for a traditional holiday piece.

wire-netting swag

NATURALLY BUT GRANDLY BEFITTING the season, this elongated swag of assorted Christmas greens, accented with fresh apples, winterberries, *Magnolia*, and red huckleberry, is constructed on a rolled-and-flattened length of wire netting (chicken wire). This method allows for a more dimensional and easily tailored design to be made with a minimum of materials.

2 Insert small evergreen tips into the wire "tube" to form the swag.

3 Using heavy-gauge wire and the hook-wire technique, wire fresh apples into the swag.

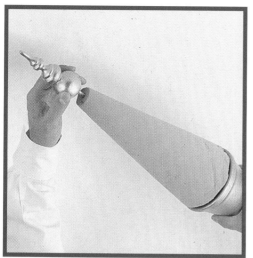

1 Glue a foam cone into a clay pot and top it with a gold, finial-like ornament.

A simple technique yields a fabulous seasonal accessory.

ribbon trees

WITH A CREATIVE DESIGNER'S TOUCH, common plastic foam cones can be transformed into delightful fabric-covered trees with an assortment of ribbon and cording. With the almost infinite selection of ribbon on the market, trees can be designed to accessorize any décor. Versatile gold-painted plastic foam ornaments do double duty as tree-toppers. These crafty creations are perfect for holiday tables, mantles, and more.

2 Crumple wired ribbon in your hands to give it a "wadded" texture.

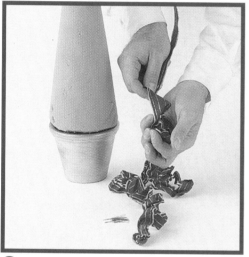

3 Wrap ribbon around the cone, pinning it as you go. Finish by wrapping with cording.

96

Create grand holiday decoratives with just a few seasonal elements.

hanging cone decorations

STANDARD STYROFOAM® CONES OFFER a number of options for designing show-stopping holiday decorations, and two exciting versions are featured here. Inverted cones, to which a "harness" of crisscrossed cording is attached for hanging, are covered with salal leaves, touched with gold leaf, and dotted with cranberries. Fresh florals arranged in an Iglu Holder (atop the cone on the right) is one option for finishing the decoration, or a bubble-bowl-enclosed candle with a collar of fresh foliage and berries is another. The possibilities are endless.

1 Coat salal leaves with spray adhesive and cover a Styrofoam® cone with them. Using black-tipped corsage pins, randomly place fresh cranberries on the cone.

2 Spray the leaf-covered cone with adhesive and randomly pat with sheets of gold leaf. Crisscross cording around the inverted cone to create the hanger. Secure with Dixon pins.

3 Glue a saturated Iglu Holder to the end of the inverted cone and arrange florals, or hot-glue a small bubble bowl to the end of the inverted cone and place a round candle inside.

1 Spray a dry floral foam cone or plastic foam cone with adhesive.

2 Roll the cone in a shoebox-like container filled with dried parsley flakes.

A creative option in tabletop trees.

parsley trees

INSPIRED BY TOPIARY ART, CONICAL forms, whether ornately or simply adorned, are among the most sought-after tabletop decoratives for the holidays. They're versatile, easy-to-place, and sure to be conversation pieces.

Reminiscent of the meticulously trimmed trees in formal palace gardens, this simple tabletop duo would make a dramatic holiday statement in a sleek, contemporary environment. Silver-painted wooden candleholders are inverted and topped with wooden eggs to become finial-like tree toppers.

3 Place the cone in a painted clay pot and top with a "finial" made from a wooden candleholder and egg.

1 Fill container with dry floral foam, allowing it to extend 1 inch to 1 1/2 inches above the rim of the container.

2 Fill a smaller container with dry floral foam as well and hot-glue it to the top of the foam in the larger container.

3 Arrange permanent materials in both containers. Tie a ribbon around the two-tiered arrangement and tie a bow at the top.

HOW-TO 98

Tiered arrangements decorate for the holidays in seasonal style.

stacked container arrangement

CONTAINERS IN GRADUATED SIZES, especially those of the same style, are perfect for use in creating multitiered arrangements. When assembled with seasonal icons and holiday treasures, stacked arrangements make an impressive presentation for holiday celebrations. Here, two sizes of bushel-like baskets, made of pickled wood, overflow with clusters of apples and sprigs of pine. A pretty plaid ribbon, tied into a bow, bundles the package for holiday presentation.

A display-size angel complemented by seasonal accents welcomes customers and attracts holiday sales.

golden angel display

A VEGETABLE GARDENER'S TOMATO cage is shrouded by a gold-painted, pleated screen to form the base of this creative display piece. The angel's head is a ball-topped finial that rests atop the cage, and the wings are formed of wire netting (chicken wire) which has been sprayed with gold paint and fashioned into a bow. Lengths of fine-quality ribbon are draped over the frame and enhanced with ribbon roses, gilded fruits and foliage, and small bunches of dried 'Million Stars' *Gypsophila*. Additional bunches of the dried baby's breath tucked into the wings add an ethereal quality to the angelic creation. Attached to the tomato cage at the back of the design are a natural twig star and halo which complete the heavenly display.

1 Pleat a long piece of wire window screen and form it around an inverted wire tomato cage. Bind the screen at the top of the cage, leaving the three prongs exposed.

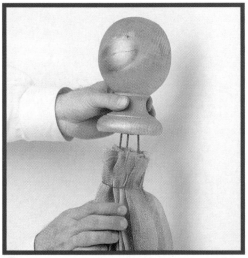

2 Drill three holes in the bottom of a wooden, ball-shaped finial and place it on top of the wire prongs. Spray entire unit with metallic gold paint.

3 To make the wings, make a six-loop bow from a long narrow strip of poultry wire. Then, flatten out the bow. Use wired cording to form a halo.

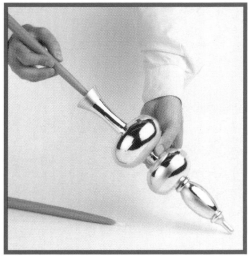

1 Insert a leftover taper into a Christmas tree-topper ornament.

HOW-TO 100

Holiday ornaments transform a seasonal floral design.

tree topper

ENHANCING YOUR HOLIDAY FLORAL designs with a few well-chosen tree ornaments is easy to do, and customers will be delighted with the results. The finished creations will be perfect for most any seasonal celebration, and with the wide variety of holiday ornaments available, such designs can be coordinated to suit a variety of color preferences and themes. Here, two gorgeous holiday decoratives, composed of vibrant red roses, sprigs of fresh pine, and permanent holly, are created with the addition of tall tree-topper ornaments. The tree toppers are supported by leftover taper candles which have been inserted into the foam that fills the containers. The floral materials are then arranged in the foam around the ornaments.

2 Carve the end of the taper into a point with a warm knife.

3 Insert the pointed end of the taper into floral foam and arrange florals.

1 Hot-glue an Iglu Holder to the center of a pedestal candle holder.

2 Arrange fresh carnations in the Iglu to form a rounded mound.

3 Place a two-loop bow of satin or velvet ribbon at the base of the carnation mound.

Stylish arrangements designed especially for ringing in the new year.

black-tie carnation arrangements

ARRANGED IN GOLD CANDLESTICKS of different heights and sizes, these sophisticated carnation creations are perfect for a black-tie New Year's Eve affair. The tallest arrangements feature mounds of white carnations arranged in foam cages and accented with black velvet bows. Bunches of *Amaranthus* burst from the center of the carnation mounds, and several stems of umbrella palm (*Cyperus*) explode in fireworks fashion. To adapt these designs to smaller centerpiece arrangements, create just the carnation puffs in the lowest candlesticks or in a flat tray and accent them with black velvet bows.